NEW AMERICAN CULTURE RACE

Jerry Unis

New American Culture Race

©2020 Jerry Unis

print ISBN: 978-1-09831-795-9

ebook ISBN: 978-1-09831-796-6

CONTENTS

FORWARD

Jerry Unis is a 30 year lawyer who resides in Orange County California. He is currently at home with his wife of 25 years and twin eighteen year old boys.

He was born in Southwestern Pennsylvania in Hopewell Township where his father worked in the steel mill and functioned as Chief of Police for more than three decades. Jerry worked in the steel mill himself between semesters in college.

After graduating from the University of Colorado, Mr. Unis moved to California to be with family and has lived there ever since.

He later attended law school and earned his JD and began practicing in California in 1987. After nearly three decades of practicing law, life's pressures urged him to stay home and care for his children while pursuing other business interests.

Having counseled thousands of individuals in legal and spiritual pursuits, Mr. Unis is better equipped than most to deal with the human spirit and psyche.

As the country proceeded through the pandemic, it became readily apparent that common sense issues were being neglected by the politicians in charge. This gave rise to the need for the book New American Culture Race. One can only hope that it is enjoyed by all. It was meant to be digested with open discourse in mind. It was not the intention that a political party be favored through the writing and reading of this book.

INTRODUCTION:
CHANGE EQUALS STRESS UNLESS AN ADEQUATE FOUNDATION EXISTS.

It became somewhat apparent to me that we are creating stress for maturing individuals because we have given them what they need to deal with the change that is inherent in modern society.

E. B. White published (sometime in 1954-55) a treatise which described our cultural evolution in dramatic yet realistic terms. He was speaking on the subject of Anthropology. Specifically cultural anthropology, when he declared that we are no longer controlling our physical evolution. As the modern technological changes were progressing at such an alarming rate that they were forcing our physical evolution to adapt to them. I am paraphrasing of course.

You see, technology was never seen as a driving force in our evolution before. It was seen as a by-product of cultural evolution. Now it has become so forceful so as to cause adaptation by us to the trends that occur in a rapid succession much like the waves in the ocean (maybe not quite that fast). Those trends that we are capable of perceiving anyway.

Without something to hold on to, we find ourselves on a ride of our lives. We simply cannot deal with this rapid technological change in a simply biological way. Therefore we are forced to drug up or religion up or to divert our thoughts away from reality all together.

This is dangerous to say the least. This may in fact be what is causing the current intellectual crevasse in the United States of America.

Just think about it. All of these great people in the greatest country that the government could support didn't all of a sudden become bad. We are still all good. We are just clinging to those great heights that we used to achieve routinely. There is no harm in that however we must solve problems as we go. Shooting at each other serves no useful purpose. Corruption has tried to fill the void to no avail.

The premise that some superior intellectual philosophy can fill this void is useful and realistic. We must however remove our prejudices regarding these philosophies and begin to analyze them anew with a realistic eye. The answers are available. We just need to have faith and hold on for the ride.

CHAPTER ONE:
NEW AMERICAN CULTURE RACE

We are being forced to adapt as a result of the Covid virus. Many things will change as a result of the stressors placed upon us and society. Store fronts may be a thing of the past. Working remotely will become the norm. We will only travel to a face to face meeting when critical elements of a deal or transaction warrant it. We will no longer greet with physical contact. Amazon is here to stay, like it or leave it. Other ways to make a living must evolve in order to maintain a free capitalistic lifestyle.

All of these changes are a result of a dramatic evolutionary force called the 'Pandemic'. Yes it is. We as a people who require security, will not change unless we are forced to change. The pandemic is the impetus this time. But other more subtle forces typically force the change with less stress but nonetheless force.

Think of how great this force is. It took the entire world by surprise. It exerted such force as to make nations move and change in order to survive (change or die). One may say that these changes are temporary. But I say that there are some remnants of that change that will stay with us forever.

Real estate sales, leasing, listing, and closing may become predominantly virtual or at least initially. The 'virtual tour' is a permanent fixture. It is yet another way to communicate the sale. Unfortunately for the overhead bean counters, it has become a largely desirable way to shop for real estate. Therefore, the virtual tour is a permanent fixture. The tour is the email of legal communication. It is yet another way to convey the property.

Travel becomes more difficult. We begin to shore up our borders. We begin to realize that the Border may be a matter of life and death for *all peoples* not just Americans.

We begin to analyze issues from a panelview and not just based upon one scientist or a particular science. We begin to distrust closeness. We emphasize physical and electronic distance as a proximity that we can trust. We understand that cultural differences must be respected and recognized.

It becomes painfully clear that we need Congressional oversight. that is not to say that we need Congress analyzing everyone else. We need to begin to analyze Congress and to question their activities, truthfulness, and direction. Small businesses are recognized as the lifeblood of our country. We Institute changes that protect small businesses. We begin to enact compromise statutes that protect small businesses and others who are vulnerable. There are many individuals, organizations and businesses that are vital to our success as a species.

There is more of a people focus as we proceed. We take time for ourselves. We begin to *value* family. We again begin to value a model that is based upon the family. We *rediscover* the family unit as a critical vehicle for the healthy survival of the species. As we do this, we recognize home as the pinnacle of import as it relates to the healthy survival of the family. In that same vein we begin to engage in Zoom meetings like never before. Leaving home less frequently may be seen as vital and healthy.

Alternative dispute resolution becomes a phrase that all consider as they seek to move forward in a positive way. Judges become a vital member of the society. Their value is rediscovered as necessary to our interactions. We begin to listen more intently. Listening becomes a 'newly discovered skill'.

All in all the pandemic will be viewed as a reset for society.

CHAPTER TWO:
ACTIVITIES THAT AFFECT US

Storefronts will become only necessary. Vacant storefronts will be a common sight. They become the site of the numerous clubs that I will describe in future chapters. Or, possibly storage facilities for retail businesses wherein their shoppers shop online. They allow the purchasers and merchants to avoid public scrutiny.

Remember I mentioned touchers and deciders. This is an example of that on a small scale. Touching the product will become relatively unimportant as deciders conclude what to buy and when after they do their online research. This concept that people make up two groups essentially is carried throughout this book.

The mail or package delivery services become very important and are used more frequently. Actual products are viewed when delivered by package delivery services and returned when subpar or when they are not what we expected them to be. This creates a responsibility by vendors to take greater care and an incentive to produce a quality product.

Most of the contact with a product or other people will occur remotely. The people who touch will begin to form cliques of one sort or another. They will start to form clubs. The individuals with similar interests will begin to find each other and use their products together or individually and or share their experiences with their clique.

The interesting part will occur when human expression becomes necessary. People will begin to express themselves on a daily basis with clothes and hair and other adornments. This is an aside but will generate a stream of commerce all its own. This is born out of the failure of retail establishments in malls and storefronts.

Observers and deciders will stand back and change less but decide more. Touchers will be the spectacle for these people and will help these people satisfy the human need to control or feel useful in some way. Observers have a big view and help the touchers to make decisions over products and the direction taken by society. Deciders must be kept in check in order to avoid outright manipulation by way of politics, elections and other forceful means.

The ruling class will become larger as capitalism is allowed and ironically they become less influential. This can be the subject of a book all alone but suffice it to say that as they become common, their thoughts and desires become passe'. This occurs unless or until the ruling class (deciders) become more numerous than touchers.

Although American culture requires no demarcation, the deciders will identify themselves through the clubs that I've described. Think of it as much like the NRA (National Rifle Association) and its political influence.

The mere fact that the ruling class becomes more numerous defeats the exclusivity of their movement. Therefore they will not dominate in American culture. Deciders are just another segment of society that have to scramble to be heard and understood. Fortunately, American dominance treats touchers equally and will soon become the law of the world. As others, (deciders and touchers) see the advantages of coexistence.

The spread of the American governance will dictate that workers become free in all lands in the world. This is what so-called "progressives" don't comprehend. Meaning that the American form of government is *progressive* for the rest of the world.

CHAPTER THREE:
LEAN AND MEAN

As a casualty or a trade off for the technological emergence in the workforce is the fact that there will be much less in the way of "extra" employees. Existing employees will be asked to do more. Multitasking is the flavor of the day. Job descriptions will be viewed with disdain by employers.

Although the overburdened existing workers will be worked to exhaustion, they will be loath to complain if they want to keep their jobs. Those that have good jobs will be in the minority. The large majority of the individuals without jobs will be left to small businesses or the government in order to survive.

The "gift" of the shut down for big business is that big business will be able to rid themselves of troublesome or unproductive employees. The employee roles will become lean and mean. Only the most productive or valuable employees will continue with the company into the future. Business will be able to do this with impunity as a result of the shut down due to the Pandemic.

Therefore, although the Pandemic is over, employment problems have just begun. The stressors created push businesses towards greater government involvement. There will be a push to create an arm of government that deals primarily with business and ensures their survival. Greater government involvement in business will be the result. Now the unemployment claims will come from businesses themselves and they will be requested to ensure that the employees that are left, benefit from that relationship with the federal government. Jobs are like gold. It is the connection that enables familial survival.

The administrative course of state and federal benefits for unemployment will flow through the workplace. This will be the most efficient method of administration for the government. This is a tradeoff in exchange for maintaining some semblance of capitalism. Otherwise, the government will control "essential business" in a communistic or socialistic fashion.

The bottom line is that this entire pandemic and shutdown will have been 'good for business'. This is much to the chagrin of so called progressives. They will try to create controversy around this relationship and encourage government takeover of the entire businesses. This becomes the new line of demarcation between republicans and democrats. The line gets thicker and longer as small businesses are consumed and dismantled. At this juncture and in this society, it would be insurmountable for any single politician alone to cross that line. No one of logical sensibilities would undertake to convert local businesses to government management and/or control. It would seem that this would be highly unpopular with the private ownership and their grass roots friends having a legitimate electoral voice.

CHAPTER FOUR:

HOW MUCH IS ENOUGH?

What emerges out of all this pressure is a new ruling class. The middle class once again becomes a force. The push back of the second amendment precludes the current ruling class from taking over in America. This creates a problem for those at the pinnacle of wealth.

Those with enough money to insulate themselves from society will realize that the *new* middle class or new ruling class is educated enough to preclude a take over by the *old* ruling class. They will realize that any attempt to take over will be met with bloodshed. They won't be able to tolerate the exorbitant price and will eventually succumb to the new junior ruling class and their existence.

The fact that many have more than enough to provide for many becomes irrelevant for a period of time. The disparity of wealth becomes a secret to be told only to family members in a discreet fashion.

Since a new class will have sufficient wealth to survive comfortably, accumulation of wealth will remain the primary goal of the new middle class. That relates to comfort for some and frustration to others. The majority of Americans will remain capitalists as the alternative is undesirable. This is because the Trump campaigns and modern transparency have pointed out the flaws of globalism.

Many will have enough and the United States will become somewhat of a ruling nation as time goes on. This of course assumes that there is no new calamity.

CHAPTER FIVE:
TOUCHERS DON'T CARE

Surprisingly, the former middle class is indifferent to the elite unless they impact the former's life negatively. The elites may attempt to influence elections as they have during the Trump era.

The manipulation that affects 1st, 2nd, 4th & 5th amendments is a gross miscalculation of the American public. These rights have been bled over and form the very basis of the American culture. Exploiting these rights is how many Americans have fun and enjoy their lives. These rights are the very essence of freedom in the United States of America.

Mark Cuban may believe that there will be uncertainty and our evolution will be slow. My vision sees an extreme exuberance due to a penned up frustration over many attempted manipulations of the American public during the Trump era. That energy will pull the public through this revolution of evolution.

Much like technology causing the evolution of society after world war two. This penned up anger will cause evolution whether temporary or permanent is yet to be seen. But the evolution will occur in a dramatic fashion. The changes that will occur, happen by a sheer reflex of the abuse suffered prior to, during and after the Pandemic.

The former middle class will cause these changes as they are more numerous and potent than the so called progressives. The lessons of this Pandemic are clear. Borders protect our freedoms and way of life. We as the United States are left to care for ourselves. No other country, state or group of countries will protect us. It is clear that we as a country were left to fend for ourselves. Even if we act as one government world wide, our voices would be far less potent than they are currently.

The former middle class will grow into their power base and realize that they have a new power that not even the wealthy elite can overcome. Therefore the FMC (former middle class) as a group largely ignores the wants, needs and desires of that particular class of people.

As humans, we are a social / herd type of species. We need each other and personal interaction is necessary. At no time is that more evident than now (post pandemic).

The act of social distancing has resulted in anxiety and desires, the satisfaction of which we previously took for granted. The deprivation of touching during the pandemic has given new meaning to the Rolling Stones "Satisfaction".

The herd mentality and our desire for physical proximity lays the groundwork for the advent of clubs in a big way. Although we have had country clubs and the like for centuries, their utility becomes clear as a result of our recent experiences.

There is a feeling of safety and security when interacting with individuals with the same wants, needs and desires. There is also a feeling of strength. The recent history has made us feel vulnerable and alone. 'Never again' say many. These sub-governments will account for their members and assure that they have a voice. This may even be the advent of the organization of clubs with other like minded clubs. The commonality may be related to survival. It may be patriotism. But, whole clubs may begin to interact to ensure strength in numbers. There may even be a common drill for an invasion of sorts.

This advent of clubs allows the individuals to feel safe and secure. It insulates them from the very wealthy so as to tolerate their existence. There is a creation and enforcement of coexistence. This allows the peace and harmony that we are used to as Americans to continue to exist. Here is the creation of class indifference. This will continue to exist as long as the manipulation by the government allows.

CHAPTER SIX:
PAPER AND POLITICS OUT. PEOPLE IN

Millennials give us the electronic record. Although the millennial generation has been much maligned, they are responsible for a significant evolutionary development. That is the dramatic decrease in the use of paper for work, play and school. Their insistence that they carry everything in one hand is a significant development.

The cell phone becomes our external brain: A bastion of knowledge. The phone is our safe which harbors our prosperity. It enables our transactions. It even helps us select our next date. Many are working on a program based in artificial intelligence that selects our next meal (a shout out to **whatz2eat.com**).

This dramatic change in record keeping creates a situation wherein current events are difficult to reconstruct. From an Anthropological standpoint, we are going back to the Prehistoric era. Unless the archaeologists are equipped with sophisticated equipment, reconstructing our era will be difficult at best. That being said, we are venturing into this era in an original way. We have really never been here before. Be that as it may, the use of paper is on the decline and may even be prohibited in the future. This will be in the name of preserving the environment.

As we have survived the virus and suffered through excruciating transparency, we are realizing that certain truths need not be obvious. The reality of politics is an exercise that many Americans abhor. We see the nuances of the truth and in many cases it is as blatant as the difference between fact and fiction. The latter creates a revulsion towards certain idealogs in the media and others in public view. We were not meant to look so closely. Unfortunately, the politics of fact vs fiction is repugnant to many.

The repugnant nature of politics disenfranchises a majority of Americans. This is unfortunate as this is a progression of an old evolutionary trend. It would seem that the impact of Corona on society merely advances this trend. However now the obvious result is to repulse many more individuals from identifying the truth.

This may give rise to a fact checking service used in conjunction with a television or other media show. Otherwise it may result in more regulation which will be difficult if not impossible to police. There are a plethora of first amendment issues to be dealt with or the enforcement will run afoul of the constitution.

Whatever the result, there is a vital need to fact check in an effort to use the media as a tool to advise and to allow us as voters to make adequately informed decisions. Many may continue to live in the fog of political rhetoric as it is easier. But most will adapt to the fact checker service as they adapted to the advent of the cell phone.

All in all, this results in a cumbersome yet accurate way to experience entertainment and news. The step will be taken by most people and will result in a meadow where a new service may thrive. It may be that channels and sources begin to fact check themselves but this is less likely if it isn't in their business plan. The sources have enjoyed the crevasse of first amendment protections for far to long. Certain restrictions thereon are justified after this era of misinformation.

One by-product of this era of misinformation is the moral justification to staunchly defend the second amendment. Does this belong here? It does because attacking the second amendment, the use of paper and excessive rhetoric regarding important issues are largely items of the "woke" disestablishment. Therefore it is important to talk about the ramifications of misusing the truth. Since the media and the democratic party uniquely assert these important factual issues in a manner that is blatantly untrue, it is reasonable to assume that if democrats take control, our civil liberties appear to be in peril. The public's only ultimate solution to the tyranny described is force of some sort. As guns are the seminal choice to exert potent force, the second amendment makes the public's case without firing a shot. But evolution says that we will if we have to.

CHAPTER SEVEN:
EVERYONE CAN LEARN

Everyone seems to agree that everyone can learn. Where the agreement falls apart is how the information is presented. We all learn in different ways. Different learning environments allow all nationalities, denominations, sexes and races to learn in a manner that is effective.

The learning environment falls apart when individual teachers are introduced that are biased or prejudiced in some way shape or form. No I don't mean prejudice in the traditional sense regarding race. I mean that a certain individual may rub a teacher the stop wrong way and the teacher will cease exuding their effectiveness towards that particular student. This type of prejudice is insidious at best and undescribable at its worst. What it does however is ensure that certain students don't learn as well as others if at all.

Covid 19 has created a calamity that may be exploited by students who don't learn as well in a traditional learning environment. The fact that remote learning has become the equivalent of daily attendance in public schools may benefit those students. Learning without fear of bias, prejudice, or even subtle personality conflicts, will result in a more relaxed setting in which to learn. One can reasonably conclude that a more relaxed student is a more productive one.

This method of teaching will certainly become more popular as a result of the forced experimentation during Coronavirus vacation. Certainly, more people will opt for a learning environment that is flexible in terms of time and duration of instruction.

SOME CALIFORNIA COLLEGES DECIDE TO OFFER ALL FALL CLASSES ONLINE

By Stephen Frank on May 05, 2020 08:48 pm

This is a big story. UCLA and other UC schools will give students a choice of on campus education or online education. To push the students away from campus, the schools are also saying they might not be able to provide housing for students. So, it makes sense to stay at home, save room and […]

The proof for this is anecdotal. The public may adopt these learning principles as being sound. In which case, a gross number of successful students will generally increase the IQ of the general populace. This lends credence to the hypothesis that the middle class will become stronger in the ensuing days and gain political clout or power as a result.

This will also bolster attendance at clubs. it will generally allow people to organize and to express themselves politically. If it is allowed to progress unimpeded, It will give rise to a system of government that is fairer and effective.

Schooling is virtual, for the best of human character. The interaction is the best that the human species has to offer sans politics. Meaning that: when human beings get together in an effort to further learning, it creates a relationship that appears to be one of the best that we have to offer. The altruistic nature of the relationship alone is something that can be applauded. Sex doesn't matter. Race doesn't matter. Sexual orientation doesn't matter. All that matters is that the material is presented in a manner that allows easy transmission between individuals. Furthermore, it will be necessary that the information being presented is current and correct. This allows for a revolution in learning. It was started with the advent of the internet and youtube. It will be given a substantial push as of its mandatory use during the pandemic.

Imagine, we can have human interaction sans politics. Two people can consult, educate, share and even teach without the distraction of the appearance of the source. The source can even offer more than one type of learning experience. It can be written, video and even audio. In the event that live instruction is absolutely necessary, a live instructor can appear for a meeting lasting not longer than the class per se. In this way theoretically the teacher may be available for many if not more students.

I would argue that the goal of educated students will be closer to 100% than would be otherwise possible.

CHAPTER EIGHT:
YOUR HEALTH COMES FIRST

Hospitals close as we migrate through this pandemic. They will never be quite so full as they have been previously. Beds may matriculate primarily based upon population growth and the greater number of serious illnesses based upon growth alone. The occurrence of disease or illness will remain essentially the same. The population may increase which will account for some bed filling.

The concierge doctor and nurse will become more common. We see the heroism of these individuals and choose to keep them closer. Practitioners will make house calls. Physicians will begin to create and maintain a patient or client list. The same patients will remain with the same doctor for years. This occurs as a result of the realization that it is a liability to go to a doctors office. All that exposure to sick individuals is detrimental to the less ill. All that exposure to younger individuals who routinely see many more. This is certainly a welcome environment for the practitioners who don't relish contacting many ill individuals at once.

Along with the difference in the practice of medicine, comes a difference in shopping for goods. Amazon has shown their effectiveness and safety through the era of pandemic transparency. Now there is much less exposure to infection, the lack of human politics and interaction for customers of delivery services. Many find this attractive and "amazon value" nearly has or achieves a moniker all its own.

Supermarket Warehouse has become common. Their delivery services copy Amazon and have Amazon value. People begin to do their own personal services. People begin to cut their own hair or have friends do it. Certainly they cannot do their own dentistry; however, they can shine their own shoes, cut their own grass, and do their own makeup. There is generally less reliance on the service industry. This may bolster the prices for the service industry. However, this doesn't do much for their roles in terms of numbers.

There is an advent of eating clubs and cooking clubs. People want to know what to expect. They also want to deal with people they know are of the same level of cleanliness. Consistency is the key. The pandemic has taught society to associate with a fewer number of people (10 or less) . This and the need for cleanliness and consistency gives rise to clubs much like country clubs. People find that these clubs need not be associated with a golf course. People find that the consistency is comforting. People also find that lower numbers are healthier for themselves and their family. There are also cost benefits to these clubs.

The cost-benefit analysis goes something like this:

The cost is that individuals will have to share their kitchen with what used to be their private home and kitchen with other like-minded individuals. The benefit is the predictable meals, cleanliness and good service. The cost is financial and sharing space as they proceed

The underlying theme of all this is that people want to know what to expect. All of the uncertainties associated with the coronavirus made that ordeal less than comfortable. People see the benefit of these small coops.

The result of all of them is that the workforce is slimmed down. The world becomes an efficient planet. People find that this may be a way to address the noisy voice screaming all the time about the environment and other uncontrollable contingencies. They can do this without sacrificing their liberty or their lifestyles. This makes it very attractive to create and maintain a workforce that is more efficient. Rather than employing so many people, robots have become commonplace. Automated assembly lines are here to stay. People get more creative in finding ways to make a living outside of a traditional job. It may very well give rise to an increase in criminal activity. There is an increase in electric vehicles and machines rather than utilizing fossil fuels. This eliminates a discharge of carbon into the environment which pleases the children of change and quiets that noisey voice that screams about the environment and other circumstances.

TV becomes a side distraction where essential facts come from other media. They may be validated or further confirmed by other sources but there's room for a change here. There is room for evolution here. A service or application that confirms actual facts is necessary due to the misinformation supplied by the media routinely. This is entirely for the new world that we have created.

We may even be slowing down. We are slowing down enough to verify the facts that the media presents. The fact that we ourselves are slowing down comes from the recognition and identification of a comfort level that is new but is a long awaited cultural norm. Prior to the pandemic, many globalists longed for a european siesta or a pace that is not quite so frenetic. We are now able to accomplish this without globalism. We identify with the people of other countries without calling ourselves citizens of the same one. We have become separate but equal. Prior to this time, many globalists would make choices in a way that was contrary to what was best for America just to make that point.

I call the new equality 'minutiae equality'. This type of equality may be somewhat difficult to comprehend. Appearances at first blush may not appear to be equal.

Our civil rights as Americans become synonymous with human rights. Our definition of Human Rights spreads to the corners of the Earth. We begin to realize that globalism is a folly left to the idealists of the day. Minutia equality applies to the sexes as well as the races.

All in all the world becomes an efficient planet. What we have created is a better world. This world is a better place to be.

CHAPTER NINE:
RELIGIOUS REVIVAL

Religion once again becomes popular. individuals understand and believe that they were given a right during the formation of this country. Those rights are believed to be God given rights and those rights are to be preserved. Religion is like the economy in that it ebbs and flows. It is because spirituality in the human race is a constant. The spiritual component of human beings is thought to be permanent as God is permanent. Even if contested by an atheist or an agnostic, there really is no denying that there is a spiritual side to most human beings that requires attention.

Like it or not God is an essential part of our cultural society. It is the reason that liberals constantly rewrite history in such a way so as to exclude Judeo Christian morals and values. Man relies on culture more and more to provide survival.[1]

Therefore Society Longs for the security of how things used to be in America. As time progresses it becomes apparent that Society is missing something that once served to provide security for us. The populist realizes the religion is missing and many run to religious religion to recapture their roots. This security (which seems imaginary to some) provides a foundation for many upon which to build their lives. Therefore many resort to religion as a way forward.

If nothing else religion provides a handbook of sorts which describes a method in which to live. This method enables one to raise relatively healthy children while continuing to function in modern society. All need not believe in order for it to be effective for many individuals.

Religion also forms the basis of relationships that are limited or that are much like another club. There are principles that promote

---

1 AJ Kelso physical anthropology second edition

honesty and integrity. There are limitations in number with small groups within the church. One member of the church can rely on another member of the church to take reasonable care dealing with important issues. These are people that you can trust with your children or pets or parents. This club is the essence of what people are looking for in a club, especially since the occurrence of the pandemic.

Priests and or ministers are typically available to facilitate human interaction. Clergyman would also oversee any possible disputes that may occur. Furthermore, there is a guide book to follow that usually results in an equitable solution (Bible). This club has nearly all things the people seek in furtherance of a healthy life for themselves, and their family.

Humans evolve and life becomes more complex; greater demands are placed on the brain. We use a greater portion of our brain as time progresses. On a greater scale we use larger portions of our brain in order to evolve. This becomes evident when we consider how man learned to walk; use a stick for a tool or read for that matter. As we learn, more and more demands are placed on the human brain which causes an awareness of sorts.[2] This awareness causes changes. The changes manifest themselves in our ongoing culture. Culture may put pressure on our biology to evolve in ways that are only discernible over time. This may mean that our stature, over time, becomes taller or that we carry more fat. There are any number of changes that can only be detected through scientific tests and others only discernible after centuries if not a millenium.

With the increase of awareness and brain size, comes even more confidence in Culture and hence religion. Although seemingly

---

2 Richard Reztak M.D., The Brain, pages 180-181

illogical, religion gains ground in terms of occurrence due to faith. Faith helped the American culture progress through the pandemic and much of it was due to a faith in the future. Although this is not technically faith in God, the lines are frequently blurred and the two are conflated. Furthermore, all of these faith type people are clumped together in one group intellectually or another club. The segregation happens in terms of information and association. The non-believers are therefore pressured to be faithful too. Sometimes it's better to switch than to fight.

CHAPTER TEN:
TWICE IS ENOUGH

Seasoned investors as well as those who dabble had to appreciate the run-up on the stock market that occurred during President Trump's first four years in office. These opportunities that existed in the stock market occurred twice due to the extraordinary occurrence of the pandemic. Unfortunately for those who weren't invested in the market, it wasn't something from which everyone could benefit.

The evolution of the stock market created a message whereby even a modest investor would take interest in the advancement of business. Certainly, they could even bet on the demise of a business in the case of a 'Down Market'. This new awareness created by the stock market forces the casual investor to look at the big picture if they are analyzing the market. This intellectual enlightenment of sorts gives rise to an awareness not previously known. One must question, whether or not this awareness stimulates evolution.

The Initial rally in the stock market was great in and of itself. It shattered many records and did things that hadn't occurred for a minimum of a hundred years. Many people benefited from a robust economy until China threw a rod into the spokes of the American economy. For many leaders that would have been the end of that initial market rally. Only someone as uniquely gifted and determined as Donald Trump could turn a pandemic into two market rallies. Those savvy investors who rode the market up and down we're able to benefit twice although the risk of an exaggerated market only occurred on one occasion. The second rally occurred nearly without risk. That is because we have experienced the heights of the market just prior to the pandemic depreciation. Since the market had been there before, we know these heights are capable of being reached.

This advantage, separate and apart from all others, may have been the greatest benefit of the pandemic itself.

CHAPTER ELEVEN:
BY INSTINCT

What has happened through the course of the pandemic is a new awareness by most. Some panic because of it. Others use it as a new instinctual awareness. It controls and affects decisions. It creates choices all its own. This is a form of evolution or change that is nearly entirely cultural, but is based upon a learned change. In the long run, it could precipitate a physical change but we have yet to make that determination. Of course, all of this is anecdotal, but, so is tax day.

We learn many things through the difficulties realized during the shut down. People begin to distinguish between tested and non-tested individuals. Actions are taken based upon an individual's decision to test. People begin to segregate or group together based upon their personal decisions in that regard. The tested people form a club of sorts. Maybe clique is a better description.

This club may go on and instigate further changes in culture or government. And so on. You can see how all of this knowledge that is based upon experience may stimulate change and hence evolution. Ultimately the society adapts to isolate carriers and unlike the shotgun approach of 'shelter in place'. We all go on to realize that comorbidity is the same as the elderly as it relates to vulnerability. We begin to carefully isolate those individuals with those conditions. Their contact is limited to tested individuals or those with no symptoms including fever. Everyone else is free to conduct their business.

This logical, rational approach will become the new norm. It becomes apparent that the pain of total isolation was unnecessary and not entirely rational. We begin to weigh the decisions that resulted in that phenomena. They begin to be put in their proper place. Never again will we shelter the general populace in place except under the most extreme circumstances.

The science experiment which was the most recent pandemic was unnecessary at best. It was foolhardy at most. Experience is a wonderful teacher. Our reaction was not entirely surprising considering that modern society had never experienced anything quite like this pandemic (incredible viral capacity and extreme contagious character).

Higher level of knowledge now possessed by Society helps us to adequately deal with future pandemics so as to allow very little disruption while protecting the truly vulnerable. We can now begin to function like we did prior to the pandemic. We begin to see how we allowed this particular issue to throw society into some amount of turmoil. There are salient facts we begin to segregate from fiction. There were different levels of truth that came out as we analyzed the pandemic and how we allowed a group of leaders to control us to our detriment of sorts.

We have yet to determine whether or not herd immunity is a critical benefit that can be gleaned from the pandemic. Therefore it may have been entirely unnecessary for everyone to wear masks. Masks may only be necessary for those individuals who are confronting the most vulnerable. It may be very useful for the rest of society to interact with each other and develop a certain amount of immunity upon low exposure to the disease. By always wearing a mask, we protect the immune system from getting stronger by systematic low-level exposure to the illness.

There certainly is no reason for individuals that have had the disease to wear masks around even of the most vulnerable. This of course assumes that these individuals have developed their immunity to the extent that they can no longer transform or propagate the virus to their detriment. We will develop an antibody test that is efficient and a treatment will become similar to a vaccine for the disease. This will cement our response to this particular pandemic into the annals of the extinct. Even though there might be a flare-up or two, we develop treatments, vaccinations and antibody derivatives go a long way to create a situation where this virus is no more lethal than the common flu.

The 'New Normal' is 'New American Culture Race'. Most people have no choice but to use this as a learning experience. The bottom line is that people understand that cultures evolve and change. The bottom line is that most people even understand that biology evolves. This becomes clear when we look at stature and how the height of people has increased as nutrition has become better in the last century.

People are much taller than they used to be. People are much smarter than they used to be. This is a result of a biological evolution of sorts. Even though biology evolves, culture evolves much more quickly.

We Begin to make future decisions based upon new cultural knowledge. There is an instinct created that I call 'New American Culture Race' human instinct. People learn to trust their instincts based upon this new cultural knowledge. Its' as 'woke' as globalism. 'The hip' are not so hip any longer. They have a new knowledge that shows them the error of their ways. Common sense must necessarily be considered when we make decisions in the future. Crowded places aren't necessarily positioned to make the best decisions for the country. Crowded places aren't necessarily the best place to foster the future of our country. Colleges and universities have become places of limited intellectual space. The revelation is that people now realize that colleges and universities are self-centered and limited in their analysis of real life. People begin to move to the suburbs and are proud to be from a small town rather than viewing that as a detriment.

Most people don't grow up in an environment where their parents teach them how to live. We teach our children math, English and science. But we don't teach them how to live. For generations now, we have relied on our school teachers to teach our children how to live. That task is onuris at best. It is unreasonable to assume that teachers will teach our children how to live. We have, for generations, burdened school teachers with the task of raising our children into becoming perfect adults. It is only logical that the teachers have begun to rebell and are pressuring the parents to do their job. This task nearly never gets done prior to college. College students appear to their professors to be empty vessels that need to be molded into whole adults. Throw in a bit of idealism for sure. And we get a picture of what the world could be if we all possessed certain characteristics and then it becomes clear why and how our children became programmed. Programmed with ideas that are impractical at best and don't serve to further our government, economy, and / or our country in general.

CHAPTER TWELVE:

THE GAP IN KNOWLEDGE
OR IS THERE?

There is a distinct arrogance by intellectuals. Shortsightedly they believe that they have cornered the market on learning. This is an error by the elite. They fail to recognize the 'school of hard knocks' as my father described it. The pressure of this learning device can be as instructive as a PHD. One only needs to be receptive to the teachers. If an individual is receptive to the lessons of life, she can learn as much as a college education if not more. There are several recent examples of life lessons learned through the pandemic that everyone has learned without the PHD.

There have been some shows of force by the police that have come to global visibility. One is welding doors shut in Wuhan, China. Another is the handcuffing of a father playing in a park with his daughter.

These shows of force were unnecessary at best and go to the root of our freedoms that we cherish as Americans. We are arrogant as American about our civil liberties. The civil liberties distinguish us from other citizens of other countries in the world. The shows of force have only gone on to redouble our efforts to preserve and maintain the Second Amendment of the United States Constitution through the Bill of Rights.

Other examples of lessons learn those individuals that lost their jobs. It becomes readily apparent through this pandemic that one does not want to lose their job unless they are to be severely disadvantaged in the future. This is another lesson college does not teach that the *common man/woman* understands.

Employers get a second look at employees through the course of the pandemic. They are free to terminate individuals that appear undesirable on the second look. The pandemic has allowed many employers to terminate employees now using the pandemic as an excuse. This further reinforces the lesson that jobs are valuable and shouldn't be lost for trivial reasons.

'Fake News' is another Common sense observation that has obvious visibility. Fake news ignores the facts. As facts are discovered the media looks worse in terms of credibility. For example, it is beyond question that China was *ground zero* and that the media misinformed the public disastrously throughout the pandemic.

We have begun to take political leaders, the news and the media in general with a grain of salt. Many had done this before, but the attitude is now even more prevalent. The sinister nature of the media has become much more obvious to the general populace and the casual viewer. This gives rise to the impetus to find alternative informational and news services.

The internet is the most obvious source of news and information. Smartphones are the source of choice for now. Individuals carefully choose their applications that provide the news and information. The gap in service gives rise to an evolution of sorts. The applications begin to carefully screen their information and news to ensure that they are credible sources of information. The public values the service and the applications begin to weed out the fake news from the facts.

This is what we have learned so far:

BORDERS

We have learned that borders are not just something that identifies patriotism. We have learned that borders are necessary in order to control an enemy that could not be heard or detected oftentimes.

TRAVEL

Travel between countries must be restricted in order to maintain a barrier when a virus or other harmful enemy or substance threatens the health and safety of the American people. This would involve immigration-reform necessarily. Although the president still has executive authority and power to act under the circumstances, we need to restrict movement in a way that it is safe for Americans and others legally visiting the country.

DECISIONS BASED UPON A GROUP OF PEOPLE

We have learned that we should make panel decisions. Decisions made by different people of different backgrounds and philosophies seem to flesh out all of the salient points that may not be otherwise discussed.

DISTRUST DISTANCE

We have come to understand that the artificial distance that we place between fellow human beings by technologies may not be a good one. We've been getting to focus more closely on interpersonal interactions as being essential to the interaction only in dire circumstances.

CULTURAL DIFFERENCES

Racism has been used as a club in the vitriol that is now known as politics. We understand now that racial differences can be used as a tool. The diagnosis and problem solving realm of society routinely uses it this way.

We begin to realize that different races have different characteristics and tendencies. We understand that different races need different solutions. Different races are not a bad thing and indeed can be positive if not essential in our everyday interaction. The differential impact of the coronavirus on Black and Hispanic populations tells us that racial recognition may in fact be a matter of life and death. Hopefully jokes and jests based upon racial differences will take on a positive note rather than being a reason for a dispute. We should develop a repertoire that will allow us to discuss these issues openly and honestly without hurt feelings or malice.

OVERSIGHT OF CONGRESS IS A NECESSITY

What was intended and what in fact exists in modern-day Congress are two different things. The framers intended that Congress would be allowed to voice their opinions that were based in Divergent yet honest feelings. What has come to exist in Congress today is a culture of 'Anything Goes'. This was not something that was intended by the framers of the US Constitution.

The framers sought to allow Congress absolute latitude to voice their honest opinions. We cannot allow the lawmaking or oversight process to devolve into a culture name-calling, dishonesty, and malice. Congress coupled with the media, is being used as an advertisement for political agenda or game. The true purpose of Congress involving lawmaking and oversight is not being accomplished through the fiction that they sell to the media in order to degrade an opposition candidate.

PROTECTION FOR SMALL BUSINESSES

We currently have a president whose heart is with the small businessman. He gives great lip service to the protections provided for small business. Effectively however he appears to be unable to protect the small business woman or man alike. It would seem that the long arms of the federal government do not go deep enough into society to reach the small business person in time in order to effectuate a positive change. The small business person will go out of business without additional help and assistance from some other local agency Etc.

COMPROMISE STATUTES

The legislators in the state and federal governments must begin to legislate a compromise when defining crimes and / or other civil disobedience. The pandemic has shown us That the circumstances of each case are different. It has shown us that frequently civil disobedience and criminal activity are the result of life-threatening circumstances. It is unjust to imprison or penalize an individual or individuals when they are faced with inevitable dire circumstances if they act reasonably. We recently had the imprisonment of a hairstylist in Texas who certainly did not deserve the sentence. We cannot allow this to occur on a regular basis or the public will lose further confidence in local law enforcement and the judiciary. This problem can be resolved by legislating a compromise into the statue that allows a modification to the results when the circumstances warrant it.

TIME FOR SELF

This reset of sorts as a result of the pandemic has given us time to stand back and gain a perspective over our circumstances. Although many of the results of the pandemic or undesirable, gaining a perspective over our circumstances should not be one of them. This allows us time to adjust and make changes. This allows time to slow down. This allows us time to stop and smell the roses. As people slow down in this regard, they realize more and more that they like it. This time for self is necessary in order to feel human. This may be one characteristic that stays with American Society for good. This also pairs us with European countries more closely. It may eliminate some of the angst that comes with capitalism. There may evolve a subculture of American society that is more relaxed than others but yet they are patriotic without being derogatory about American culture.

NEVER LEAVE HOME WITHOUT IT

Zoom meetings are now commonplace. There are individuals who described Zoom meetings as essential to conducting everyday business. Sometimes in fact it involves individuals never getting out of their seat to discuss an issue with a comrade that is in the same office. Other times it involves a meeting with an individual on the other side of the world. The Zoom meeting is a much more effective tool then either a telephone call or a text message. Inside, it is much more effective than an email. As much as I hate to layer another form of communication over those which we already have, the zoom meeting appears to have created and occupies a communication niche now all its own.

ALTERNATE DISPUTE RESOLUTION

As lawlessness becomes more and more commonplace people look for ways to resolve their disputes without the involvement of law enforcement. Mediators become more and more commonplace. Cultural Chiefs begin to resolve neighbor disputes in such a way to keep the peace. The justice of the peace may make a comeback. This low-level forum of administration seeking justice may now become commonplace. In the practice of law there is intense interest surrounding agencies that resolve disputes alternatively. The niche is a welcome one for frustrated lawyers and those who see advocacy as predominantly one-sided. The public embraces these mediators and they are held in high esteem by the populace that they help.

LISTENING CAREFULLY BECOMES A SKILL

As we realized that interpersonal interaction is important and cherished, as we learn to listen ever more carefully. Individuals begin to understand that their own happiness is dependent upon others. Emphasis is placed upon listening as a skill. mothers listen better. Fathers listen better. Children who want their way begin to listen better. The mediators that were previously described must possess team listening skills in order to survive and be successful. Listening may even be taught as a class virtually. Zoom facilitates these listening characteristics as there is a delay after a person speaks so that the Listener can respond. This may even result in a dispersion of individuals more evenly across the country. Especially with the Advent of the 'zoom meeting' and the other virtual ways to do business.

PARTICULATE MATTER IN THE AIR IS NOTICEABLE

As travel is on the decline and people don't commute as frequently to work, the LA Basin becomes clearer.It is noticeable that the sky is cleaner. The air is clean. The new level cleanliness is embraced by many. Even those automobile enthusiasts must admit that the air is cleaner now that there are less commuters. The by-product of the commute can easily go away without much in the way of objection. It certainly calls for stronger efforts to capture the carbon deposits in our biocarbon exhaust. It may not result in the demise of the internal combustion engine but it is a result that is desirable. We should antic-ipate many efforts in the future to keep the air as clean as it is.

THE ELECTORAL COLLEGE EQUALIZES

Many begin to realize that there are several advantages to living out-side of the city. Thankfully the founding fathers anticipated the dif-ferential of voice vote and the need for the Electoral College. rather than give in to the crowds on the coast and the deranged voice that it creates, people will begin to spread out across the country so as to have a more comfortable life and to maintain an effective voice vote. we will soon realize that there is very little downside to living in the country and that in effect it may be ultimately more enjoyable. It is certainly slower and more comfortable for those that like that pace. The equalization of the population between the coast serves to save the small business person. It also rescues the small towns from dissolving. Their ancestors are saved by the new blood and ideas of their children. The children see that they can maintain their ances-tral family while continuing to engage in a dynamic and robust busi-ness. All of these tools allow a very positive impact from coast to coast without sacrificing the popular vote and American fairness.

WHAT WILL REFLECTION REVEAL?

Time will determine the other lessons to be learned from this pan-demic. My crystal ball isn't entirely clear on this issue. Suffice it to say there will be unexpected consequences both good and bad from the pandemic. Being an eternal optimist, I say that we will have many more positive developments as we evolve into the future.

CHAPTER THIRTEEN:
LUCKY THIRTEEN

The 13 original colonies had their beginnings under Queen Elizabeth I and saw its first permanent settlements under King James I of England. They would begin in Jamestown and eventually spread across the entire Atlantic coast, with exception of Florida.

Each colony had its own founder and own set of ideas and each tended to be formed from outcasts in English society. The Puritans of Massachusetts Bay fled persecution, the Quakers of Pennsylvania did the same as did the Catholics of Maryland.

The result would be 13 original colonies with an independent mindset that would realize itself in the American Revolutionary War.[3]

Although I have long been a proponent of random selection, as the population becomes more disciplined and evolves, there is an attraction to the American characteristics of bravery, integrity and intelligence. This is a deliberate selection by human beings and causes society to evolve in a significant way. As society evolves in this way it becomes clear that there is a distinct American nationality. Many might not like what it is, but there is definitely an identity that is American.

There can be no dispute, that our identity demands recognition and respect. The fact that we look out for Americans first isn't selfish. It is healthy self interest. The detachment exhibited by individuals who criticize this self interest are nothing more than those possessing a shallow juvenile awareness that someone is in need. The maturity occurs and their opinion changes when they are confronted with some depth on the issue. This grows into a mature culture that is on equal footing with the rest of the world. This cultural awareness is

---

3 Russell Yost February 9th 2012

somewhat advanced by what was learned throughout the pandemic. This should be the definition of 'woke. '

The colonists from the 13 colonies had a tendency to possess characteristics that included honesty, intelligence, bravery, possessing Integrity, fiercely Independent, and freedom-loving. One cannot deny that this created an independent genetic line selected to thrive in the "new world". These individuals known as Americans did not like to be told what to do. Governmental control was something that they took great measures to avoid. They risked their very lives. They risked their families. They risked their wealth. They founded a country based upon the ideology that they could practice freely what they believe without hurting anyone else.

This Society that was created still exists today as the United States of America. There are many people that failed to contribute. There are those that came to America after the great price was paid that are attempting to undermine this genetic line. The true patriots of America abhor to allow any erosion of the original Constitution and its spirit.

The 'original thirteen colonies' has independent cultural significance. The significance is that these people possess the aforementioned traits selectively and genetically. Beyond the individual, these traits are embedded in their genetic identity. Therefore the evolution of these individuals has created a patriotic genetic line all its own. This is not to say that these individuals own these characteristics. This is just to say that these characteristics have been isolated in a certain portion of the United States of America when they were created in the original 13 colonies.

This is significant because adversity impacts this genetic line of individuals in a different way. This group of individuals respond to adversity in a different way than those individuals that lack these characteristics. They have a tendency to be more confrontational. They have a tendency to be more determined. They have a tendency to be more resilient.

It is significant to say that these characteristics define the American genetic line. Certainly others with these characteristics (immigrants). Mostly these immigrants admired those characteristics before coming here and chose America because of these characteristics and traits. These individuals that chose America eventually become American if desired.

The individuals that live here that don't possess these traits feel left out or discarded by the silent clique that understands the patriotism that consumes the United States of America. If one can be convinced to embrace American patriotism and embrace the ideology which allows this pandemic to be an advantage rather than a defining moment, they can help unite the country rather than engaging in this political vitriol that defines us today.

With this comes a cultural society that is somewhat advanced. We are now a society that questions everything not just authority. It could be that 'authority' has obscured itself but for efficiency's sake I will use the 'questions everything' as the moniker.

CHAPTER FOURTEEN

NATURAL SELECTION BREEDS FOR SUCCESS

As previously stated, I have long been a proponent of random selection, as the population becomes more disciplined and evolves, there is an attraction to the American characteristics of bravery, integrity and intelligence. This is a deliberate selection and causes society to evolve in a significant way. As society evolves in this way, it becomes clear that there is a distinct American nationality.

A different type of intelligence is recognized. 'Redneck country stupid' is thought of as an *independent thinker. Groupthink* (or *sheep think* as I call it) is thought of as blind or ill-conceived. The group think mind set is characterized by identification or association with a group or a club. This would include a political party, a particular race, or color or national origin. This may even include characterization according to sex. We are blind to any ideal that we take for granted as being true without exercising serious analysis. This is true of many of the so-called progressives.

On some occasions, there may be less direct pressure today to evolve. This indirect pressure creates a captive anxiety. The avenues to work become somewhat more limited than previously. Regulation precludes that which would otherwise be viable businesses. As mentioned before, this gives rise to the creation of black and/or gray markets within which to function. There is definitely direct pressure to create a laissez faire attitude as it relates to crime and civil disobedience. This occurs on both political sides for different reasons.

As a way of coping in California, most of the locals ignore the law. They seek to 'get away with things'. This is the California way.

How is it that we did not recognize this for so long? We are still a young Nation. We are still growing. We are still learning and changing. We are establishing our identity and culture as Americans.

As we recognize how incompetent, deceitful and inept government officials have become, we trust less and less and take on the burden information gathering. This becomes a serious endeavor that is nearly necessary in order to survive. Therefore each family or individual has an information gatherer that rises to a level of importance in that particular family or going concern. We all realize the necessity of information in our daily lives and note that a failure in any information may result in dramatically different living as well as dying conditions.

How does this affect physical evolution? It is anyone's guess. Possibly, a sophisticated geneticist has the ability to link the traits associated with Americanism. Certainly the choice of those traits are subjective. It would be a difficult study to run with certainty. Lets just leave the end of this treatise as the point that America has a nationality and that culture has been affected by this Pandemic in a positive way from an evolutionary standpoint.